015

P9-DTD-889

DAMIAN, MY SON. This digital document contains multiple data layers for your access only. Each section provides a high-level overview of my methods, strategies, allies, and enemies, as well as my motivations for taking up this crusade. Terabytes of additional data on each of these subjects are stored in the Batcomputer for further review as needed.

As Batman, I must be prepared for any eventuality, including my own abdication. Though I do not expect this file to be activated for many years to come, when the time arrives it is my wish that you shall become Batman.

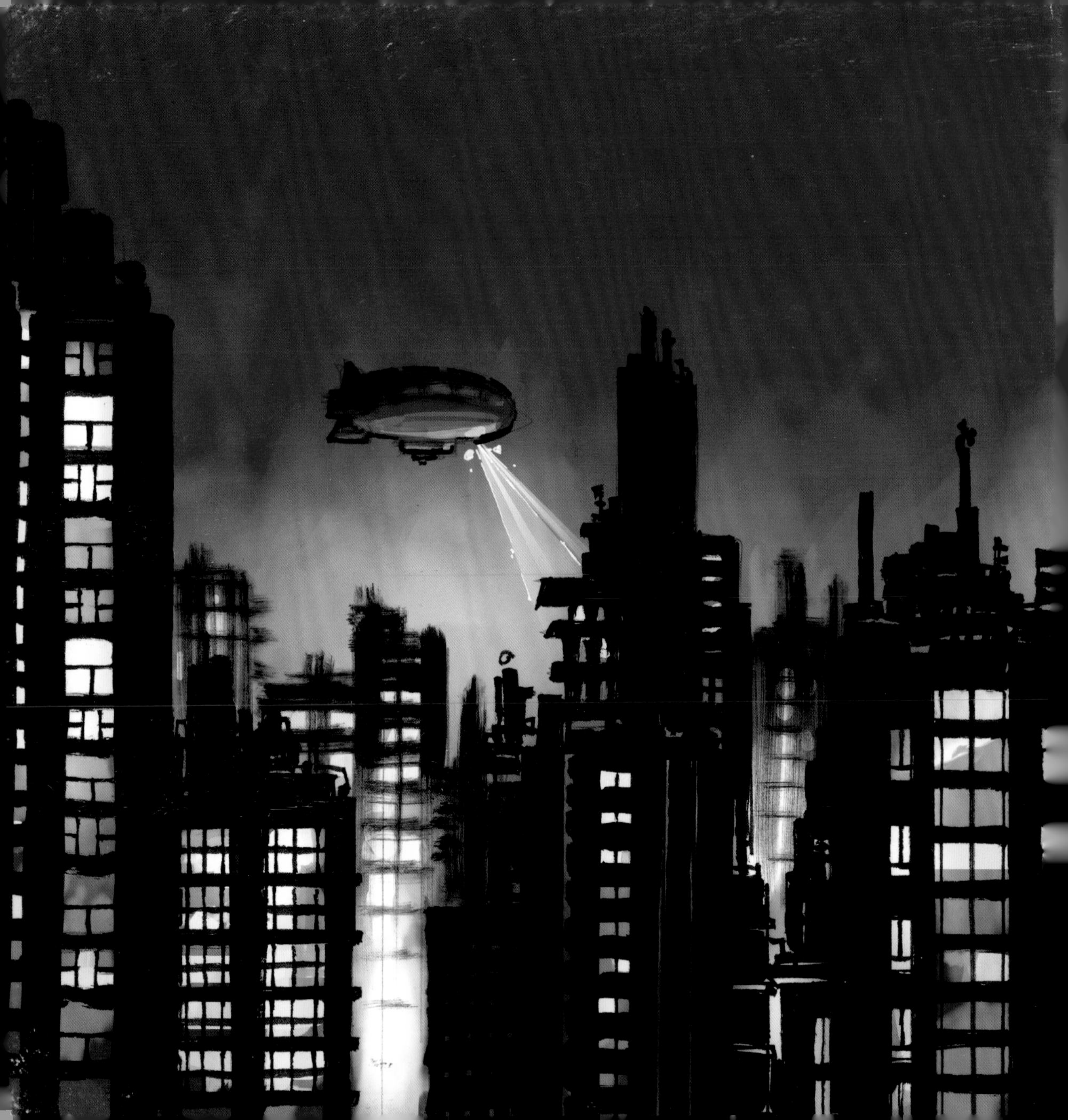

THE WORLD ACCORDING TO

BATMAN

Written by
DANIEL WALLACE

Illustrated by
JOEL GOMEZ
AND
BETH SOTELO

INSIGHT ◉ EDITIONS
San Rafael, California

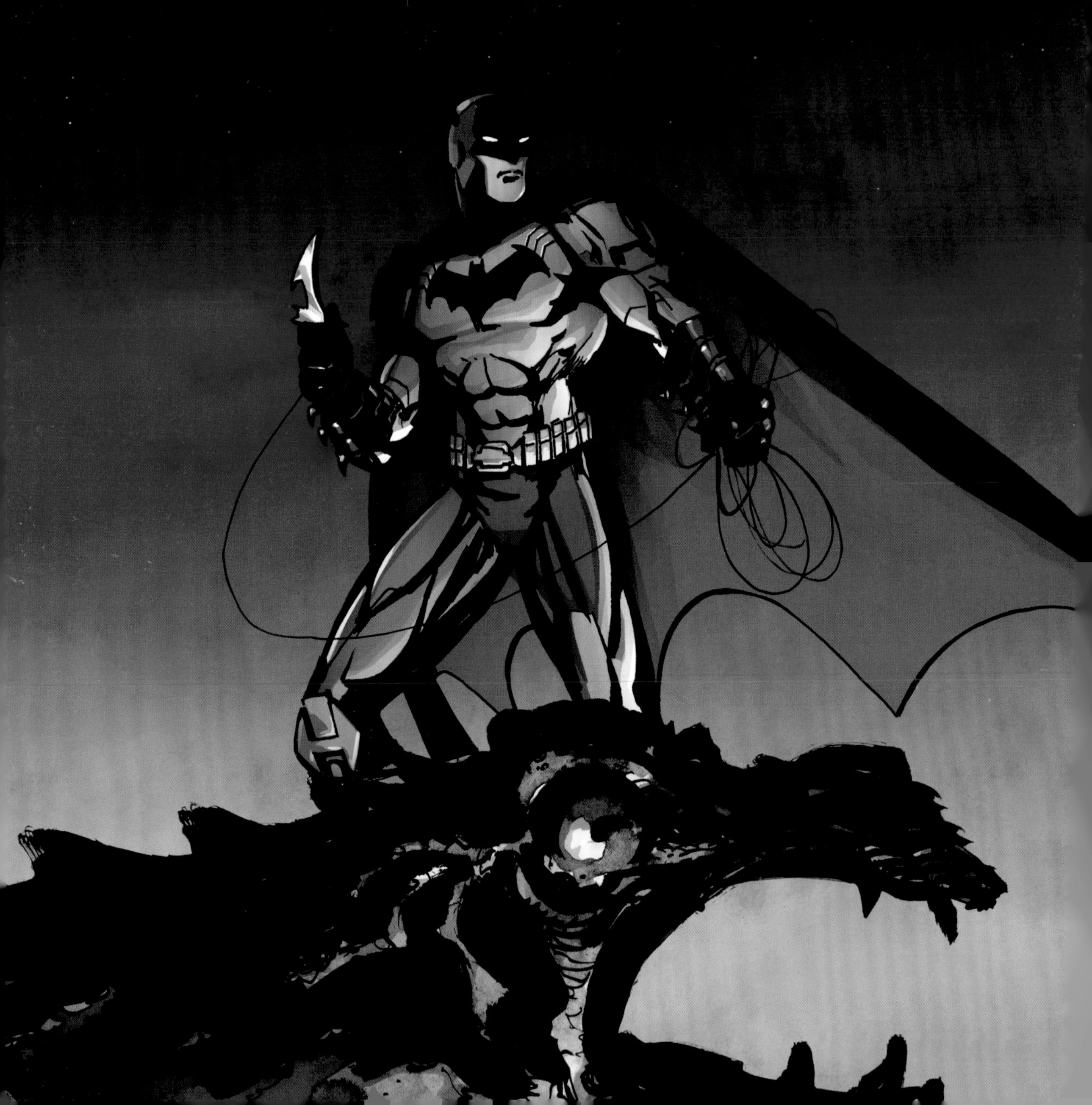

CONTENTS

WHY I FIGHT

I HAD EVERYTHING as a child—money, privilege, education. But in one moment, my life became one of loss.

Billionaires gunned down by a common thug. The papers had a field day. They painted it as rich vs. poor, but that has always been a distraction.

The true fight is for justice. It's what allows order to prevail over chaos. Civilization has moral laws. They supersede the laws written by the courts. Those are the laws Batman enforces. This is the code *you* must now enforce.

NAME:
Pennyworth, Alfred

BACKGROUND:
Former field medic (British Army), former actor

SKILLS & EXPERIENCE:
Butler, surgeon, mechanic, impersonations, armed and
unarmed combat training

As you know, Alfred raised me until I reached the age at which
I could travel the world to train for my war on crime, and
afterward he was there to welcome me home. Alfred has been
there since the beginning and knows everything about Batman's
operations. He is your most valuable resource. You cannot do
this job without him.

PREPARATION

MY PARENTS were great philanthropists. But money couldn't save them from a killer's bullets.

If I wanted to save others from the same fate—if my goal was to prevent children from growing up lost and alone—I could not afford to keep my distance from across a boardroom table. I couldn't stay safe. I no longer deserved that luxury.

Chemistry. Criminology. Forensics. Psychology. I studied all of them, learning what I could without caring about a paper degree. These are the fields that explain why and how crimes occur, and they provide the tools to catch those responsible.

These fields are never static. Always assume you have more to learn. Pursue additional studies when you're not on patrol.

Judo. Tae Kwon Do. Capoeira. Krav Maga. Fencing. I identified combat masters in each discipline and sought them out wherever they made their homes. The Wayne fortune helped open doors, but these masters would have expelled me had I failed to demonstrate my conviction at any time.

Although you have trained extensively with the League of Assassins, you must also be willing to enter into a limited-duration apprenticeship at one of these combat schools if you find your skills slipping. You may feel you already possess sufficient fighting skills, but these masters can teach you patience, emotional discipline, and the value of mercy.

PRIMAL POWER

I CAME BACK to Gotham City a changed man. Yet not changed enough. My first patrol, I hit the streets at night in the most dangerous part of Gotham City. I looked the part—a random tough in street clothes. Yet I still felt like a rich kid dressing down to go slumming. I tried to break up a burglary. The criminals fought back—confident, coordinated. They were not afraid of me. You know better than to repeat my mistake.

I had the skill, but I lacked power. How, then, could I harness fear? That night, as I sat aching from a hundred bruises, it crashed through the window of the drawing room.

The monster I had glimpsed as a boy when I had fallen into the caves beneath the mansion. *The bat.*

On some level, the creature still frightened me. But now I could harness that feeling and make the bat my own. And once I had achieved that, I could project that same fear onto the superstitious and the cowardly.

That night, I became a bat.

This psychological power is what feeds the legend of Batman. At the time, I understood it only dimly on an unconscious level. For your benefit I am now making it plain.

I used the shape of the bat to craft a symbol that would fill the criminals of Gotham City with dread.

THE BATSUIT

THE COSTUME STARTED WITH A SILHOUETTE. A flowing cape would conceal my body's contours, making me difficult to target. Dark colors would allow me to vanish into nocturnal shadows. The cowl had the pointed ears of a bat, and a bat's outstretched wings adorned my chest.

I didn't look human. I looked vampiric, animalistic—and hungry. It was an early design. The costume was slapdash and vulnerable. It could have gotten me killed.

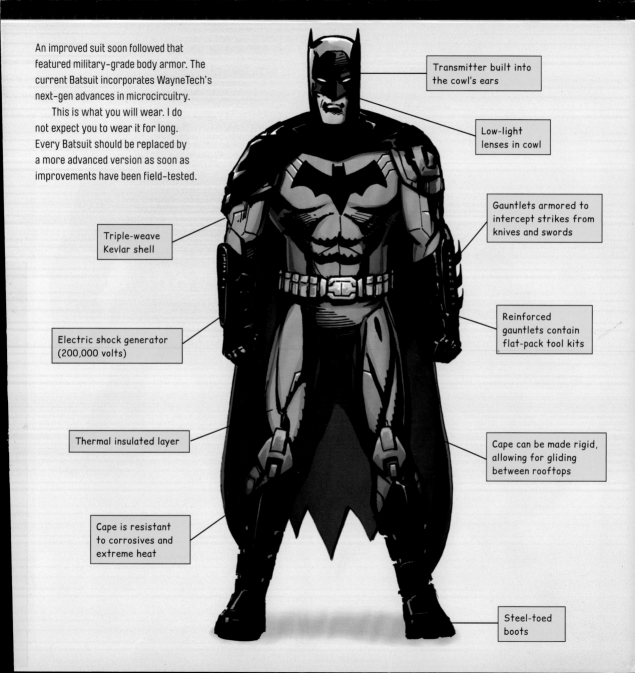

An improved suit soon followed that featured military-grade body armor. The current Batsuit incorporates WayneTech's next-gen advances in microcircuitry.

This is what you will wear. I do not expect you to wear it for long. Every Batsuit should be replaced by a more advanced version as soon as improvements have been field-tested.

Transmitter built into the cowl's ears

Low-light lenses in cowl

Gauntlets armored to intercept strikes from knives and swords

Triple-weave Kevlar shell

Reinforced gauntlets contain flat-pack tool kits

Electric shock generator (200,000 volts)

Thermal insulated layer

Cape can be made rigid, allowing for gliding between rooftops

Cape is resistant to corrosives and extreme heat

Steel-toed boots

BATSUIT VARIANTS

FIRST BATSUIT

One of my first designs, this suit was abandoned in favor of one that incorporated more body armor. It featured gloves only—no gauntlets—and its padded sleeves and pant legs created a ribbed look. For this suit, I experimented with a supplemental Utility Belt strapped to the right thigh.

THRASHER BATSUIT

This high-tech armor served its purpose when I battled Gotham City's secret society, the Court of Owls. It is insulated to operate in subzero temperatures. Its pointed-tip gauntlets split open to reveal additional weapons and electronic countermeasures.

JETPACK BATSUIT

The twin-turbine jet pack is capable of near-silent hovering yet can rapidly ascend to a flight ceiling of more than 10,000 feet. Its rigid wings are used to maintain midair stability and control flight direction.

HAZMAT BATSUIT

Designed to be 100 percent impervious to environmental contaminants, the Hazmat suit has a sealed, pressurized interior and a triple-filtered breathing mask. Useful against foes who use gas attacks including Scarecrow, Poison Ivy, and the Joker.

ESSENTIAL TOOLS

BATMAN DOESN'T HAVE METAHUMAN ABILITIES, though it suits me to let criminals believe otherwise. The rumors are outlandish: Batman can phase through the steel wall of a sealed vault. Batman can teleport in a flash of smoke. Batman can summon a cloud of bat familiars from the netherworld in a swirling, shrieking whirlwind.

Exaggerations are to be expected when so few know the trade secrets. The truth? Non-traditional problem solving and applied theatrics. You are familiar with the basic operations of these tools, and therefore you understand the importance of being prepared.

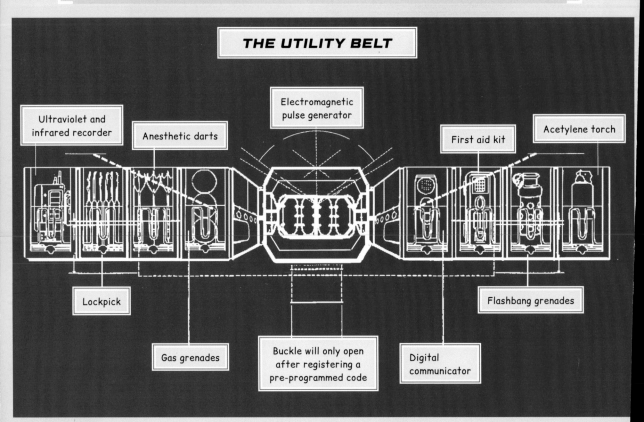

THE UTILITY BELT

Ultraviolet and infrared recorder

Anesthetic darts

Electromagnetic pulse generator

First aid kit

Acetylene torch

Lockpick

Flashbang grenades

Gas grenades

Buckle will only open after registering a pre-programmed code

Digital communicator

GRAPNEL GUN

This launcher fires a grappling hook attached to a jumpline. As soon as the hook has secured firm purchase, the jumpline reel rapidly retracts and pulls you to that spot in mere seconds.

BATARANGS

Batman's signature weapon. I have invented many models. You must have several of each type on hand at all times:

- **THROWING BATARANGS** are the standard model, designed for distance and long, arcing trajectories

- **HARD-IMPACT BATARANGS** are blunt-force throwing weapons

- **CUTTING BATARANGS** feature micro-serrated edges

- **EXPLOSIVE BATARANGS** incorporate a timed delay before detonation

NONLETHAL TAKEDOWNS

BATMAN WILL NEVER CARRY A GUN, and Batman will never kill intentionally. End of discussion. Even the worst criminal has a future. Batman will not take it from them.

Nonlethal combat is a difficult art—one that requires discipline and focus. To excel at these techniques, you must be among the best fighters in the world and able to switch combat styles on the fly if you find yourself outmatched.

As alternatives to firearms, these weapons can be used to take out foes from a distance. Other options are knockout darts and gas grenades.

STUN GUN

- Stored on Utility Belt; fires darts attached to conducting filament
- Delivers electrical charge to induce neuromuscular incapacitation
- Use only at distances less than 40 feet and only against targets with non-insulative armor

BATARANGS

- A boomerang throw will arc and return to your hand
- An overhand knife-throw will bury the weapon's sharp tip in your target

GRAPNEL GUN

Grapnel is designed to grip building edges but can also be used in combat:

- Fire and allow claw to attach to target
- Retract cord to pull target in range

PERSONAL COMBAT

THESE ARE THE CENTRAL TENETS of Batman's combat style.
Build upon these principles to develop a hundred variations.

HARD TECHNIQUE

- Counter your opponent's moves with equally forceful moves of your own

- Use low kicks aimed at the opponent's legs to upset balance or injure joints

- Use medium blocks aimed at the opponent's arms and midsection to disrupt their attack

SOFT TECHNIQUE

- Deflect your opponent's moves passively and use their momentum against them

- Don't meet an attack with a block, but redirect their energy away from you

- With the attacker off-balance, pin them to the ground with a throw

REMOVING ENEMIES AS THREATS

- Use sleeper holds and stunner blows to the back of the head to temporarily incapacitate opponents without lasting injury

- Tie up incapacitated foes with cord on Utility Belt

THE BATCAVE

ONCE I MADE MY MARK ON GOTHAM CITY, I needed space to operate—somewhere close to home that could remain undetected by the curious. The natural caverns beneath Wayne Manor offered everything I needed. I cleared out the debris, rigged them for lighting, and transformed the space into a headquarters for Batman's war on the criminals of Gotham City.

The Batcave is simultaneously a vehicle garage, repair bay, police laboratory, gymnasium, hospital, and trophy room. An underground river provides direct access to the city.

In recent years I have collected fewer mementos, but those that remain on display are symbols of Batman's early cases. You may wish to begin acquiring trophies of your own.

ROBOTIC TYRANNOSAURUS REX

ACQUIRED: After case involving Gotham City's Dinosaur Island amusement park

OVERSIZED PROP OF 1947 PENNY

ACQUIRED: After capture and arrest of Penny Plunderer

CASE CONTAINING ROBIN UNIFORM (JASON TODD)

ACQUIRED: Placed in Batcave as memorial following Jason's death

OVERSIZED JOKER PLAYING CARD

ACQUIRED: Brought to Batcave for analysis during early Joker case

VEHICLES

BATMAN NEEDS TO GET TO A CRISIS before it spirals out of control. That means speed, which requires the use of vehicles. You are inheriting these, so understand that they can be dangerous if you haven't logged enough hours behind the wheel or in the cockpit. Ask Alfred to customize the driving simulator if you need practice.

As you replace these models with upgraded versions, remember that they must be unique yet should not be traceable back to the Wayne family or Wayne Industries. They must also be armored, technologically superior, and intimidating in design. Criminals should feel dread when they see you approaching. Each of these vehicles is a visual signature announcing "Batman is here."

BATMOBILE

Voice-activated and self-driving. You can direct the Batmobile remotely, misleading criminals as to your whereabouts.

BATWING

Supersonic low-orbit flight ceiling that will enable you to cross the globe in hours. Vertical take-off and landing (VTOL) engines allow the Batwing to hover in place or touch down without requiring a runway.

BATBOAT

Pincer manipulators. User gauntlets in cockpit control external claws to aid in underwater search and rescue.

BATCYCLE

Gyroscopic stabilization. When activated, cycle cannot tip over, even at speeds in excess of 200 mph.

THREAT ASSESSMENT AND DIVERSION

BY NOW, most criminals know they cannot hope to beat Batman in a one-on-one fight. Instead they seek to even the odds by arming themselves or by banding together in packs. This is how you should deal with both tactics. Determine the composition of the threat. This includes the number of foes, their estimated combat skill, level of situational awareness, and the presence of weapons.

Use Batarangs to create a distraction or to knock out enemies from a distance.

Use the environment to your advantage. Separate the members of the group and eliminate them one by one.

Prioritize your targets. Take down armed foes first, as well as any enemy with the capacity to raise the alarm. Save unarmed or inexperienced foes for last.

If hostages are involved, they must always be your first priority. Isolate them from the action and remove them from the line of fire.

As the group is whittled down, the remaining enemies will become confused and agitated. Use this to your advantage.

If the situation gets too intense, disappear with a smoke-grenade burst and use a grappling hook to lift you to higher ground. Use this time to reassess your options before engaging again.

WAYNE INDUSTRIES

WAYNE INDUSTRIES BANKROLLS Batman's war on crime, but the company represents a much broader force for good for the people of Gotham City and the world as a whole.

As Bruce Wayne, I am president and CEO of Wayne Industries. I take its legacy seriously. The company carries the name of my mother and father, and it will continue to honor them after I am gone by carrying out good works and effecting institutional change.

WAYNE INDUSTRIES

Diverse, forward-thinking—and profitable! The latest fiscal quarter has seen Wayne Industries advance on all fronts. Under the leadership of CEO and chairman Bruce Wayne, the company has expanded into new international markets and made huge strides across all business units.

The various divisions of Wayne Industries including Wayne Technologies, Wayne Medica Wayne Aerospace, The Wayne Foundation, Wayne Chemical, and Wayne Shipping, ensur that the company is represented in a wide varie of arenas, helping to realize Wayne Industries goal of making the world a better place.

WAYNE
INDUSTRIES

ANNUAL REPORT
HIGHLIGHTS

WAYNE TECHNOLOGIES

Robotics, cybernetic interfaces, virtual holography, and microcircuitry are just a few of the innovations recently unveiled by WayneTech, with many more on their way into the consumer electronics market. Wayne Technologies' ability to study and reverse-engineer any device ensures that no innovation will fail to find a law-enforcement or consumer application.

WAYNE MEDICAL

Wayne Medical continues to lead Gotham City's healthcare industry through heavy investment in hospital infrastructure and cutting-edge research and development programs. Breakthroughs in genome sequencing from the Wayne Biotech division offer a promising glimpse of a future without chronic illness.

WAYNE AEROSPACE

Its private jets and airliners continue to make Wayne Aerospace a stellar success year after year, and the company has recently signed new contracts for defensive military applications. Details of the contracted vehicles are still top secret, but these advanced aerial designs are in it for the long haul.

THE WAYNE FOUNDATION

A beacon of charity to those who need it most, the Wayne Foundation continues the work of the late Thomas and Martha Wayne by providing food, shelter, and medical care for Gotham City's least fortunate citizens. Through free clinics and educational assistance, the Wayne Foundation is actively working to eliminate poverty and bring hope to the less fortunate.

USE DAYLIGHT WISELY

BRUCE WAYNE IS MORE THAN JUST MY PUBLIC PERSONA. That identity is a vital component of my fight against Gotham City's crime and corruption. You will enjoy a similar front-facing, highly-placed corporate position within Wayne Industries. I have arranged for it. Use this role to work cases from different angles and to surreptitiously question suspects. You may be surprised to learn how freely people reveal their true intentions in the comforting light of day.

MAKE APPEARANCES

Gotham City's elite social scene is a busy one. If you don't participate, your absence will be noted. Rely on Alfred to weed out the redundant and less notable invitations. Make it your goal to attend multiple society events each month. At a garden party, regatta, or charity auction, your primary purpose should be to glean information from guests. These are figures with their fingers in politics, shipping, technology, and the stock market.

Many of the attendees will be slightly intoxicated, impairing their judgment. Play along by drinking nonalcoholic ginger ale out of a champagne glass.

It isn't uncommon for Catwoman, the Riddler, or another costumed thief to interrupt a gallery opening. Keep your gear nearby and be ready for action.

INVEST IN GOTHAM CITY'S INNOVATORS

The next generation of Gotham City inventors requires funding. By meeting with them, you will be in a position to evaluate the potential of their work. Hopefully, your early intervention will steer the next potential Mad Hatter or Mr. Freeze onto a more positive path.

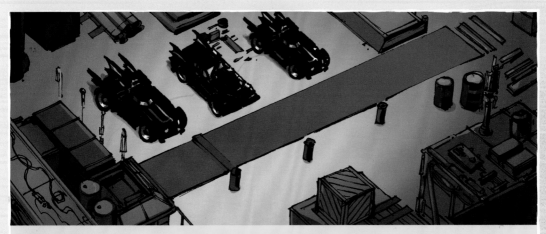

KEEP R&D FULLY FUNDED

WayneTech's Research and Development department is vital to the company's continued profitability and to Batman's success as a crimefighter. A top-secret skunkworks lab—publicly unacknowledged by Wayne Technologies—works with advanced materials to produce technology that reduces crime and improves lives.

BATMAN IS NOT the only one fighting to preserve this city. The officers of the Gotham City Police Department stand on the front lines in the battle to keep the streets safe.

Not every cop is trustworthy. Corruption is a contagion. It's not unique to Gotham City, but it breeds freely here.

But there are many you can trust, starting at the top.

POLICE COMMISSIONER JAMES GORDON

Gordon does not see Batman as a loose cannon who needs to be stopped, but as an ally whose reach extends beyond the jurisdiction of the G.C.P.D. Gordon brought in his own handpicked crew after he became commissioner, making a clean break with the corrupt administration of his predecessor.

DETECTIVE RENEE MONTOYA

Montoya has an eye for detail and an understanding of how Gotham City's costumed criminals operate. She is not intimidated by Batman's reputation and will challenge you if you try to claim priority at a crime scene investigation.

DETECTIVE HARVEY BULLOCK

Bullock is sloppy, loud, and seems to exist on cigars and coffee. He is also one of the best cops on the force. Bullock is loyal to Commissioner Gordon and can be counted on to aid Batman.

THE BAT-SIGNAL

It was Gordon who installed the Bat-Signal on the roof of Gotham Central. Its beam projects a bat-symbol on the underside of low-hanging clouds or across the vertical concrete of a skyscraper. Its activation also triggers a coded alert, simultaneously picked up by the Batcomputer, Batmobile, and a receiver on the Utility Belt.

Gordon switches on the Bat-Signal whenever he's looking for help. Or when he just needs to talk. Don't overlook this resource. Responding to the signal as quickly as possible is a top priority. Every year there's a petition to remove the Bat-Signal. Some call it "government endorsement of vigilantism." But Jim Gordon ignores them.

GOTHAM CITY

THIS IS MY CITY. The Waynes have called it home for more than 150 years. Even though you were not born here, you must make it your own. I know every inch. I maneuver from above, using a grappling line to glide between rooftops.

The alcoves of Gotham City's gothic architecture are drenched in shadow. Few people ever look up. Those who do—their night vision contaminated by street lights—can't see me in concealment. No window stays sealed to me. No secrets remain hidden.

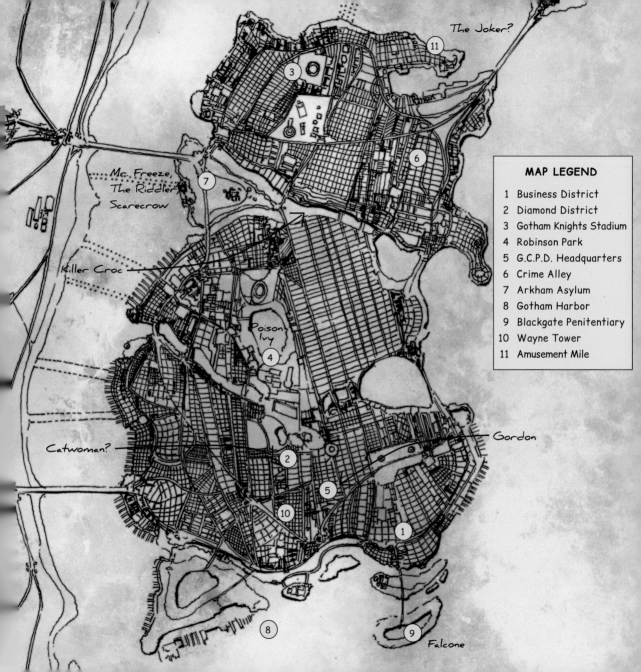

The Joker?

Mr. Freeze,
The Riddler,
Scarecrow

Killer Croc

Poison
Ivy

Catwoman?

Gordon

Falcone

MAP LEGEND

1 Business District
2 Diamond District
3 Gotham Knights Stadium
4 Robinson Park
5 G.C.P.D. Headquarters
6 Crime Alley
7 Arkham Asylum
8 Gotham Harbor
9 Blackgate Penitentiary
10 Wayne Tower
11 Amusement Mile

ROBIN: THE FIRST RECRUIT

I AM NOT raising an army for my war on crime. But I do need allies. And, if you are reading these records, you know that, ultimately, I require a successor.

Dick Grayson was the first. He had been orphaned by criminals seeking to put the squeeze on the circus that employed his parents.

I knew the pain of losing those you loved, and I knew the path to overcoming that pain. Dick became Bruce Wayne's ward and Batman's apprentice. He became Robin.

As you know, he would later take on my mantle for a time with you at his side as Robin.

DICK GRAYSON

He started with a unique skill set. Raised as an acrobat, he possessed flexibility and aerial agility astonishing in one so young. As Robin, the bright colors of his costume mirrored his origins as a circus performer. Irreverent but never careless, Robin became my partner. The media loved it. In time, Robin learned all he could under my guidance. Seeking independence, he built his own heroic legacy as Nightwing.

JASON TODD

Jason Todd was my second recruit. I thought I could apply the same approach I had used the first time, not taking into account Jason's troubled mental state. The Joker killed him. A Lazarus Pit restored him to life and he became the Red Hood—taking on one of the Joker's former identities. After his resurrection, Jason's addled mental state led him to seek revenge on me. He is now an ally, but be careful that he doesn't become an adversary.

TIM DRAKE

Unlike my previous enlistees, Tim Drake came to me. An accomplished detective, Tim came close to determining my double-identity. He wanted to train, and his athletic ability and computer skills made him a viable candidate. Tim took the identity of Red Robin. He currently works with the Teen Titans.

DAMIAN WAYNE

You, Damian, are not the first in this role, but you have undergone more intensive instruction than any of your predecessors. You spent your first decade in your mother's care and began training in combat techniques the day you could walk. Your skills far outstrip my own at the same age, and you will be an even greater hero if you can control your impulses for violence and vengeance. Once you take up the mantle of Batman, do not be afraid to seek out the advice and support of Dick, Jason, or Tim.

GOTHAM CITY'S UNDERWORLD

WHEN I FIRST STARTED OUT, Gotham City's crime scene wasn't exactly the madhouse it is today. But "organized" crime is no less malicious. Murder, extortion, exploitation, and bribery paralyzed the city. Everyone knew it—from the mayor to the former police chief—and most of them profited from it.

The Falcones. The Maronis. And dozens of lesser families who operated under their protection. I set out to dismantle their hierarchy, and I started at the top. And for that, I needed help.

I collaborated with police lieutenant Jim Gordon and district attorney Harvey Dent to take them down. Batman found evidence that the G.C.P.D. couldn't touch. Gordon's cops followed up on my leads, busting dozens of criminal rings across the city. Harvey waged war in the courtroom and put mobsters away—proving that order still reigned in Gotham City.

The mob families aren't broken, just . . . quiet. Keep an eye on them.

Felice Viti

Carla Viti

Mario Falcone

Johnny Viti

Lucia Viti

Gaetano Viti

Romano Viti

Carmine Falcone

Louisa Falcone

Alberto Falcone

Sofia Gigante

Rocco Gigante

The Falcone family ruled
Gotham when I began my fight.
Many of its members are still
active. They secretly pull the
strings behind many super-villain
plots, so stay alert.

Vincenzo Gigante

Luigi Gigante

THE JOKER

ONCE I BROKE the crime families' hold on Gotham City, costumed villains arose, many of them physically scarred, most of them psychologically damaged. It all started with him.

It was one of my earliest cases. After hours at the A.C.E. Chemical Company. I broke up an attempted robbery. The leader of the Red Hood gang, his face concealed beneath his helmet as he fled, tripped and plunged into a chemical vat. No body was ever recovered.

Was this him? Was this the Joker? How can such a psychopath have remained undetected until his first crime? Where were the warning signs?

THE JOKER IS demented but brilliant. He is a skilled electrical and mechanical engineer and a world-class chemist, despite no evidence of formal training.

He is deceptively strong, extremely limber, and possesses an absurdly high tolerance for pain.

The Joker has themes he returns to again and again: clown gags, amusement parks, playing cards, and brightly painted airships. But that doesn't mean he's predictable. I have studied the Joker more than any criminologist on earth, and every time I think I've figured out his next move, he does the opposite.

There are, however, two certainties. He wants to put on a show, and he wants Batman to be his guest of honor. Inevitably, the Joker will make himself known and unveil his latest scheme for the benefit of Batman. The trick is stopping him early enough to prevent the deaths of innocents.

Acid-squirting flower:
Defense: Use your cape as an acid-resistant shield

Gag pistol that fires BANG flag as spear:
Defense: Stay low; the gun aims high and he only gets one shot

Electrical hand buzzer:
Defense: Intercept with armored gauntlets; they are insulated and will diffuse the charge

BANG!

I have assembled a sampling of the Joker's most notorious cases. Study these and gain insight into how he thinks. Your perspective might be the thing that finally breaks the deadlock between Batman and the Joker.

CASE FILE | JOKER TOXIN

SUMMARY: One of the Joker's earliest cases saw him poison prominent Gotham City citizens with his newly-invented gas, one that contorted the faces of its victims into haunting grins. He also employed a surprising gift for disguise, impersonating a police officer assigned to a high-profile security detail.

NOTE: The Joker is deadly, even if he doesn't appear to be carrying a weapon.

The Joker's Crimes

NOTE: The Joker could be anyone. Don't assume you're hunting a colorful clown.

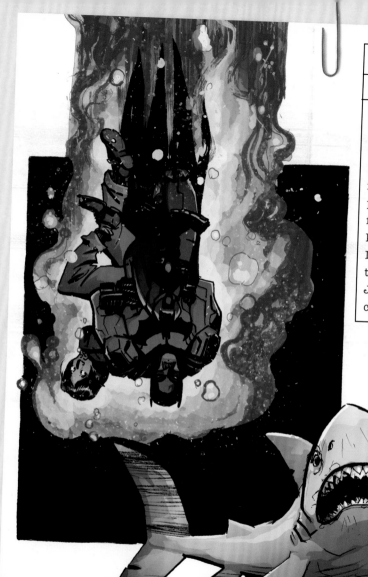

CASE FILE

FIVE-WAY REVENGE

SUMMARY: After escaping incarceration, the Joker sought out the ex-henchmen whose testimony had led to his capture. I identified five targets but arrived too late to prevent the Joker from murdering four of them. But the Joker knew I was tracking him. When I caught up to the final victim at the Gotham City aquarium, the Joker dumped us both in a tank containing a man-eating shark.

NOTE: Don't rush in without full knowledge of the risks. Especially in a hostage situation.

CATWOMAN

SELINA KYLE can be an ally, but I hesitate to call her a friend. We share a physical attraction but are both too guarded to establish a true bond of trust. Catwoman has remarkable agility and an unmatched knowledge of Gotham's City's alleyways and penthouses. She is also an unrepentant cat burglar who specializes in breaking into high-rise apartments and slipping past museum security. Despite this, her heart is usually in the right place.

Selina maintains numerous aliases and is equally comfortable mixing with slum dwellers and millionaires. In acrobatics and agility, she surpasses even me. Don't think you will be able to catch her in a rooftop chase. That's what she wants you to believe, and that's when she's probably leading you into a trap.

NOTE: Be wary of Catwoman's claw-tipped gloves. She also carries a whip that can entangle any pursuer.

POISON IVY

DR. PAMELA ISLEY interned at Wayne Botanicals before an accident altered her DNA. Genetically, she is a plant–human hybrid. She would cast humanity into the ocean if it benefitted the growth of her beloved plants. Poison Ivy often utilizes deadly toxic lipstick and her special abilities include telepathic control of plant life and the release of mind-controlling pheromones.

NOTE: Harley Quinn and Poison Ivy are close. The more Harley can be removed from the Joker's presence, the more improvement I expect to see in her mental well-being. Her evolving appearance and shifting allegiances can be turned to your advantage. It is not too farfetched to think that Harley could become an ally.

NOTE: Use nasal filters on cowl at all times when facing Ivy. Never let her make direct contact with your skin.

HARLEY QUINN

DR. HARLEEN QUINZEL studied the Joker at Arkham Asylum and fell under his influence. Reinventing herself as Harley Quinn, she convinced herself she was the Joker's sidekick and love interest. The Joker doesn't always agree. Quinn is a world-class gymnast with surprising upper-body strength.

TWO-FACE

HE'S KNOWN AS TWO-FACE, but I don't call him that. His name is Harvey Dent. I believe that Harvey is still reachable inside that monster. Batman will save him, even if I must leave the task to you. He is my friend, and I will not abandon him.

It was the three of us—me, Jim Gordon, and Harvey—who teamed up to take down the Gotham City mob. As the newly-elected district attorney, Harvey had earned a reputation as Gotham City's golden boy. He also acquired the nickname "Apollo" for his good looks.

Jim operated within the law; I operated outside it. Harvey wielded the law's full force to put the city's worst gangsters behind bars.

TWO-FACE'S TRADEMARKS
Watch for these signs:
-Use of double-barreled shotgun
-Henchmen who are identical twins
-Crimes committed at the time of 2:22
-Crimes committed in February

Harvey's two-headed silver dollar. If the scarred side comes up on a coin flip, Harvey chooses the harmful action. When it doesn't, he acts like the man I once knew.

TWO-FACE

HE'S KNOWN AS TWO-FACE, but I don't call him that. His name is Harvey Dent. I believe that Harvey is still reachable inside that monster. Batman will save him, even if I must leave the task to you. He is my friend, and I will not abandon him.

It was the three of us—me, Jim Gordon, and Harvey—who teamed up to take down the Gotham City mob. As the newly-elected district attorney, Harvey had earned a reputation as Gotham City's golden boy. He also acquired the nickname "Apollo" for his good looks.

Jim operated within the law; I operated outside it. Harvey wielded the law's full force to put the city's worst gangsters behind bars.

TWO-FACE'S TRADEMARKS
Watch for these signs:
- Use of double-barreled shotgun
- Henchmen who are identical twins
- Crimes committed at the time of 2:22
- Crimes committed in February

Harvey's two-headed silver dollar. If the scarred side comes up on a coin flip, Harvey chooses the harmful action. When it doesn't, he acts like the man I once knew.

POISON IVY

DR. PAMELA ISLEY interned at Wayne Botanicals before an accident altered her DNA. Genetically, she is a plant–human hybrid. She would cast humanity into the ocean if it benefitted the growth of her beloved plants. Poison Ivy often utilizes deadly toxic lipstick and her special abilities include telepathic control of plant life and the release of mind-controlling pheromones.

NOTE: Harley Quinn and Poison Ivy are close. The more Harley can be removed from the Joker's presence, the more improvement I expect to see in her mental well-being. Her evolving appearance and shifting allegiances can be turned to your advantage. It is not too farfetched to think that Harley could become an ally.

NOTE: Use nasal filters on cowl at all times when facing Ivy. Never let her make direct contact with your skin.

HARLEY QUINN

DR. HARLEEN QUINZEL studied the Joker at Arkham Asylum and fell under his influence. Reinventing herself as Harley Quinn, she convinced herself she was the Joker's sidekick and love interest. The Joker doesn't always agree. Quinn is a world-class gymnast with surprising upper-body strength.

Harvey's relentless pursuit of those who considered themselves Gotham City's kings had already driven him to the edge. When a vengeful mob boss splashed acid in his face, the disfigurement finally pushed him over.

SCARECROW

Dr. Jonathan Crane understands, as I do, the psychology of fear. But he cheats. Crane's fear gas operates on the brain's amygdala region and induces hallucinations. Victims experience their worst nightmares.

NOTE: Cobblepot is well-connected and always listening. It is often more advantageous to let him operate, observing his comings and goings so that he can lead you to bigger fish.

THE PENGUIN

The Cobblepot family has roots in this city rivaling those of the Wayne family, but Oswald Cobblepot is an unworthy heir. The Iceberg Lounge is a restaurant, nightclub, and casino on the Gotham City waterfront. It serves as the Penguin's legitimate front. Insecure, he believes his idiosyncrasies to be proof of his uniqueness. His fixations include:

- Formal dress: Tuxedo with tails, top hat, monocle
- Birds: Primarily penguins, but also cassowaries, emus, flamingos, cockatoos, and numerous songbirds kept in a private aviary
- Umbrellas: Variations include a bulletproof model, flamethrower model, helicopter model, electrified model, dart-shooter model

NOTE: Despite his claims, Scarecrow is not fully immune to his own fear gas.

THE RIDDLER

Edward Nigma is an expert at creating and solving puzzles. He cannot let an intellectual challenge pass without solving it. Nor can he commit a crime without intentionally leaving clues behind. Use both flaws to outwit him.

NOTE: If he thinks you're taking too long solving a puzzle, the Riddler may provide you with additional clues.

BANE

Raised in a Santa Prisca prison, Bane prizes strength through combat. Don't underestimate him. Bane is no bruiser, but an elegant tactician. A constant drip of Venom steroid boosts his strength and healing.

You will hear that Bane is the one who finally "broke the Bat." Not true, but my recuperation from spinal injuries sidelined me for months. Don't let Bane wear you down. Don't

MORE THREATS TO GOTHAM CITY

KILLER CROC

Waylon Jones. Afflicted with atavism causing reptilian mutations and enhanced strength.

WEAPONS: None, but possesses sharp teeth and claws.

WEAKNESSES: Has few physical weaknesses but can easily be outwitted. Avoid fighting Killer Croc in water.

CLAYFACE

Basil Karlo. Former actor transformed into a shapeshifter.

WEAPONS: None, but capable of mimicking anyone's appearance after contact with the target's DNA. He can also shape his limbs into clubs and spikes. Because Clayface can squeeze through small gaps, ensure that any containment unit is airtight.

WEAKNESSES: Invulnerable to attacks with blunt and edged weapons. Limited vulnerability to flames and explosives. Highly vulnerable to extreme cold.

HUGO STRANGE

Psychologist who deduced Batman's secret identity as Bruce Wayne.

WEAPONS: Syringes with mind-altering chemicals.

WEAKNESSES: Strange's mind has supposedly been purged of sensitive knowledge, though I cannot say if this is permanent. Note that even if I am no longer wearing the cowl, the revelation of Wayne Industries' ties to Batman could prove devastating.

MR. FREEZE

Victor Fries. Cryogenics expert obsessed with restoring a frozen woman to life.

WEAPONS:
- Freeze gun. Coats target in ice and reduces molecular motion.
- Containment suit. Maintains subzero body temperature.

WEAKNESSES: His well-being is dependent on his suit. Rupturing the suit will force Freeze to retreat to cooler surroundings.

RĀ'S AL GHŪL

The "Demon's Head." Leader of the League of Assassins. And your grandfather. Unlike most of Batman's foes, Rā's al Ghūl has a truly global reach. His aim is to restore the planet's natural balance by exterminating most of its people. You are not likely to outlive him, for he is immortal. Be warned that he and Talia may try to lure you back into their world.

WEAPONS: Rā's al Ghūl is an expert swordsman whose prowess with the blade presents a considerable challenge.

WEAKNESSES: His immortality depends on his so-called Lazarus Pits. Destroy these and Rā's al Ghūl's power evaporates.

TALIA AL GHŪL

Your mother and Rā's' daughter and heir, should he ever elect to cede control of the League of Assassins. Talia and I have been close in the past. But we have spent most of the years since our first meeting as enemies.

WEAPONS: As you know, Talia was trained by the League of Assassins to use a wide variety of weapons and is an expert with both firearms and close-combat weapons.

WEAKNESSES: Despite her ruthless streak, your mother has a tender side that sometimes weakens her resolve.

COMBAT CASUALTY CARE

LACERATIONS

CAUSE: Very common in this line of work, particularly at the hands of knife-wielding maniacs like Mr. Zsasz.

TREATMENT: Apply constant pressure to stanch the bleeding, with a sterile dressing if possible. If there is any loss of sensation or motor function, consider applying a pressure bandage or tourniquet. When bleeding has stopped, irrigate the wound to dislodge contaminants with disinfectant saline.

ELECTRICAL SHOCK

CAUSE: The effects of the Joker's joy buzzers depend greatly on the type of current used, the voltage, and the point of contact.

TREATMENT: Activate the Batsuit's biomonitors to ensure that the electrical current has not triggered involuntary muscle contractions or arrhythmia, which can lead to cardiac arrest. For electrical burns, refer to the section on burn treatments.

FROSTBITE

CAUSE: Sustained exposure to extremely low temperatures within Mr. Freeze's ice blocks, particularly on bodily extremities such as the hands, feet, nose, and ears.

TREATMENT: Warm the affected areas slowly with water or temperature-controlled gel. Do not treat if there is still likelihood you will soon be exposed to frostbite conditions again, as this can damage tissues.

IN THE EVENT OF INJURY, you must be able to tend to your own wounds. First aid kits are stored in the Batmobile and in miniaturized form on your Utility Belt. These will all be used and often. The most common injuries you are likely to sustain on patrol are listed here, along with on-the-spot field treatments you should employ until you are able to return to the Batcave. Alfred is a former battlefield medic and can continue your treatment once you are safe.

BROKEN RIBS

CAUSE: Chest trauma through blunt force or compression, such as the bear-hug squeeze of Killer Croc.

TREATMENT: Ice the ribs to reduce swelling and bandage for support, but do not bind the chest tightly due to risk of lung collapse. Ribs will heal naturally in less than two months. Wear a suit with added armor until then. Avoid direct combat if possible as further damage could perforate internal organs.

BURNS

CAUSE: Unprotected exposure to jets of flame, encountered in the Gotham City refinery or when battling the criminal Firefly.

TREATMENT: A third-degree burn penetrates all skin layers and can cause muscle damage. Don't remove your armor until you are safely back at the Batcave, but cover the area with a sterile dressing until then. Beware the risk of carbon monoxide poisoning through smoke inhalation; when in doubt, use the rebreather on your Utility Belt.

POISONING AND ANAPHYLAXIS

CAUSE: Poison Ivy's airborne pollen and pheromones can trigger life-threatening allergic reactions.

TREATMENT: Evacuate the area at the first sign of contamination, even if the Batsuit's respirator shows no signs of a breach. Toxins may be absorbed through the pores instead of via inhalation. Be wary of any difficulty in breathing or any swelling of the face or throat. Hives, itching, and blistering are common symptoms of Ivy's most virulent concoctions. If it's a contact poison, flush the exterior of the Batsuit with decontaminant spray.

ARKHAM ASYLUM

ARKHAM ASYLUM has stood since the early 1900s. For most of that time, it has earned its label as a madhouse.

Named for founder Amadeus Arkham, the facility has remained in family hands ever since. Jeremiah Arkham is its current administrator. Arkham Asylum is notorious for unsanitary conditions and cruelly excessive methods of treatment. Few patients are ever cured. Many grow worse during their stay.

The sheer number of villains kept within these walls makes Arkham Asylum a target. Criminals on the outside frequently try to free their compatriots—sometimes by smuggling items inside, sometimes by breaking through the asylum's concrete walls.

BLACKGATE PENITENTIARY

Gotham City's only maximum security prison facility. Prisoners who aren't judged to be insane by the courts—the Penguin, for example— are sent here to serve out their sentences. Located on an island in Gotham Harbor, Blackgate features countermeasures that dampen the abilities of superpowered inmates.

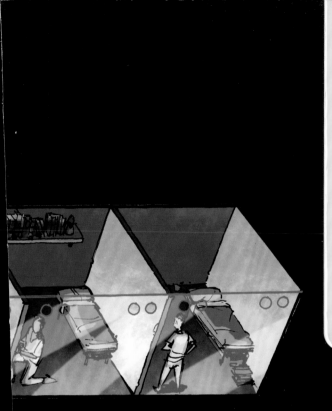

METHODS OF INVESTIGATION

AS A CRIME FIGHTER, you must be a skilled combatant. But more important, you must be an expert detective.

COLLECTING CLUES

Every crime scene tells a story, and not all clues are as plain as those left by the Riddler. Criminals leave behind fingerprints, skin flakes, and sweat droplets. You might find abandoned tools, gunpowder residue, and physical evidence speaking to the skill of the criminals and their ultimate intent.

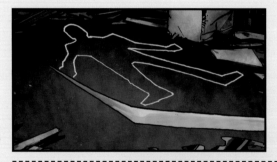

OBSERVING

Most of the hours you spend in the Batsuit will be devoted to watching, listening, and waiting. During stakeouts, you may remain motionless on a rooftop for hours, scrutinizing your target's movements through your cowl's night-vision lenses and recording conversations with the parabolic audio collectors built into the Batsuit's cowl. Your target will run out of patience before you will.

DEDUCING

With serial offenders, it isn't enough to determine how they pulled off their last crime. You must anticipate where they'll strike next. Using all the information you have gained so far, put the pieces together to understand your enemy's modus operandi.

GOING UNDERCOVER

Bruce Wayne as big-spending celebrity is not the only persona I play. Years ago I infiltrated Gotham City's criminal ranks as "Matches Malone," and in this guise I heard things I could not gain through intimidation. Develop and nurture your own aliases.

ANALYSIS

The laboratory in the Batcave features the most advanced forensic equipment in the world. If you learn of a new invention in the field of criminal science that you do not possess, invest in it.

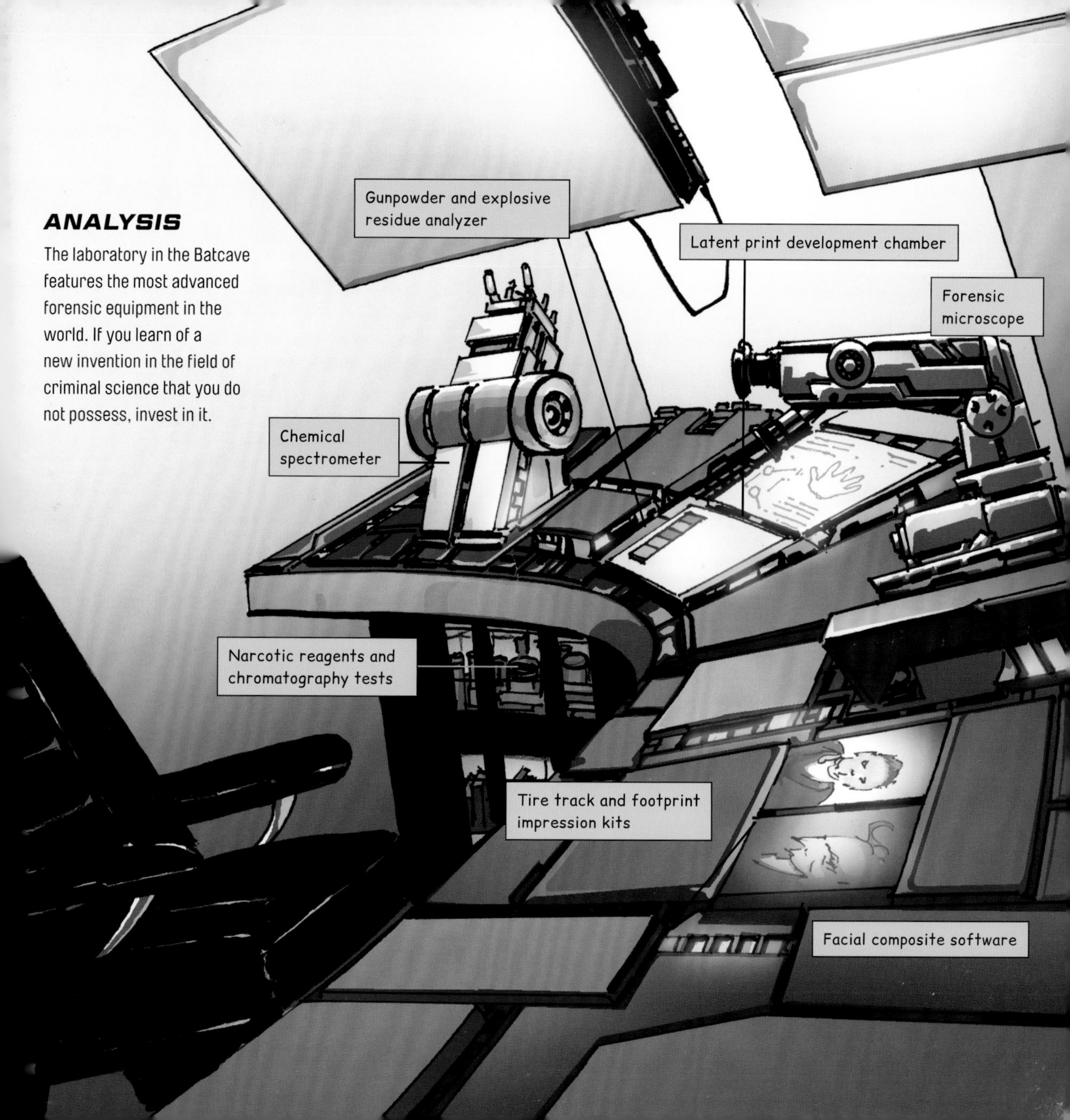
Gunpowder and explosive residue analyzer
Latent print development chamber
Forensic microscope
Chemical spectrometer
Narcotic reagents and chromatography tests
Tire track and footprint impression kits
Facial composite software

ASSEMBLE THE FACTS

WORK MULTIPLE CASES SIMULTANEOUSLY. Look at every clue from a different angle. Seemingly unrelated facts might be part of something larger. Get the big picture before the conspirators make their move.

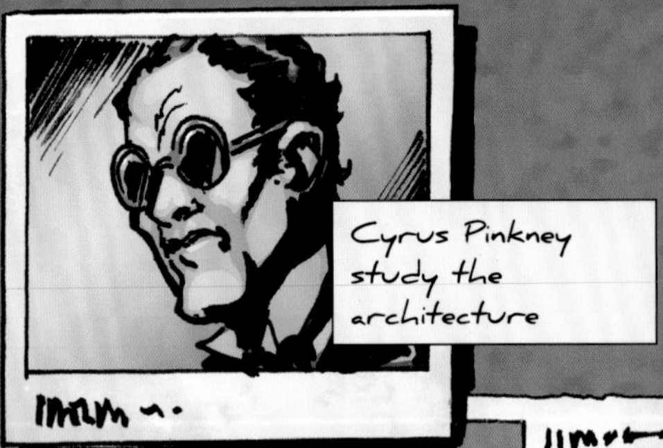
Cyrus Pinkney study the architecture

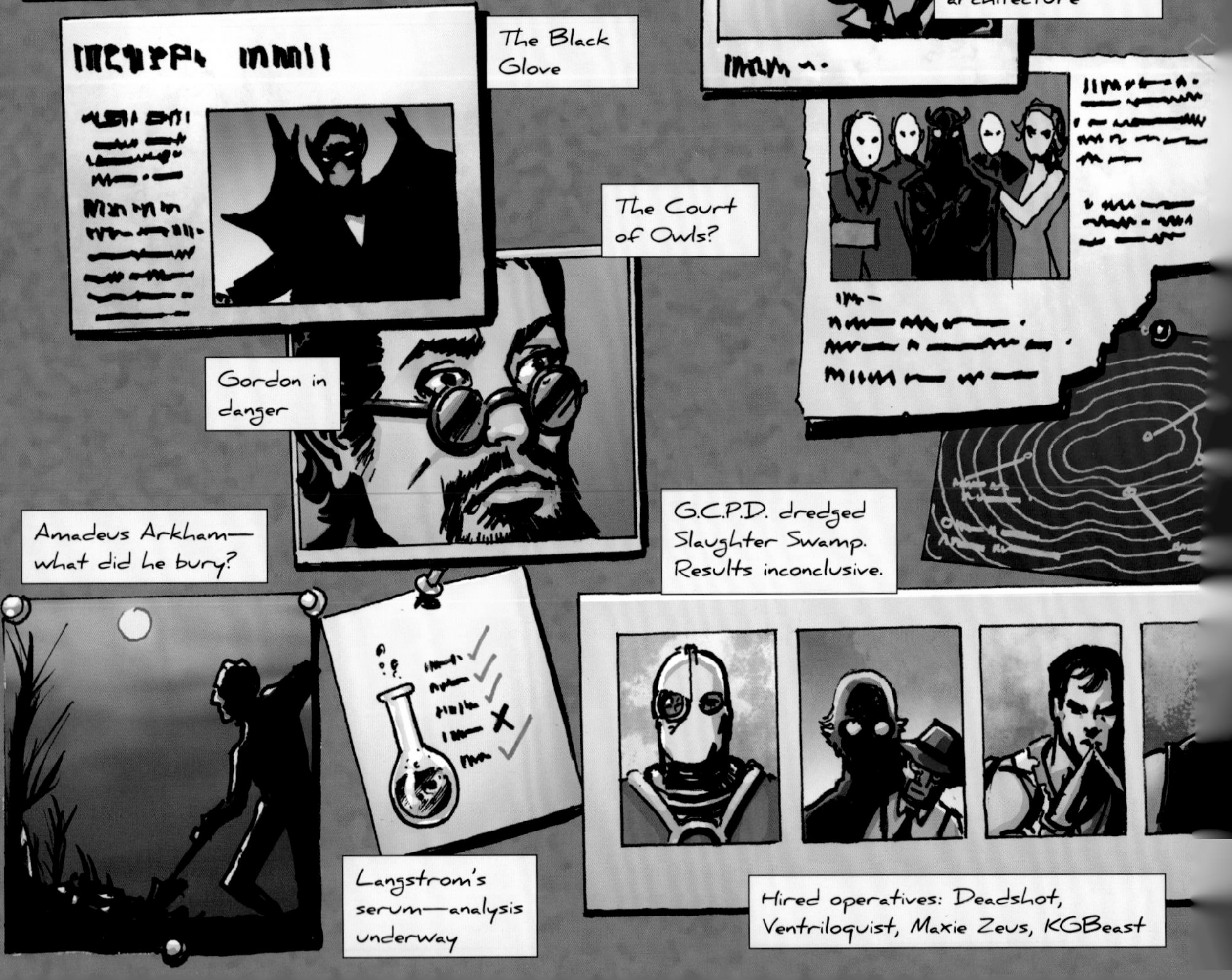
The Black Glove
The Court of Owls?
Gordon in danger
Amadeus Arkham—what did he bury?
G.C.P.D. dredged Slaughter Swamp. Results inconclusive.
Langstrom's serum—analysis underway
Hired operatives: Deadshot, Ventriloquist, Maxie Zeus, KGBeast

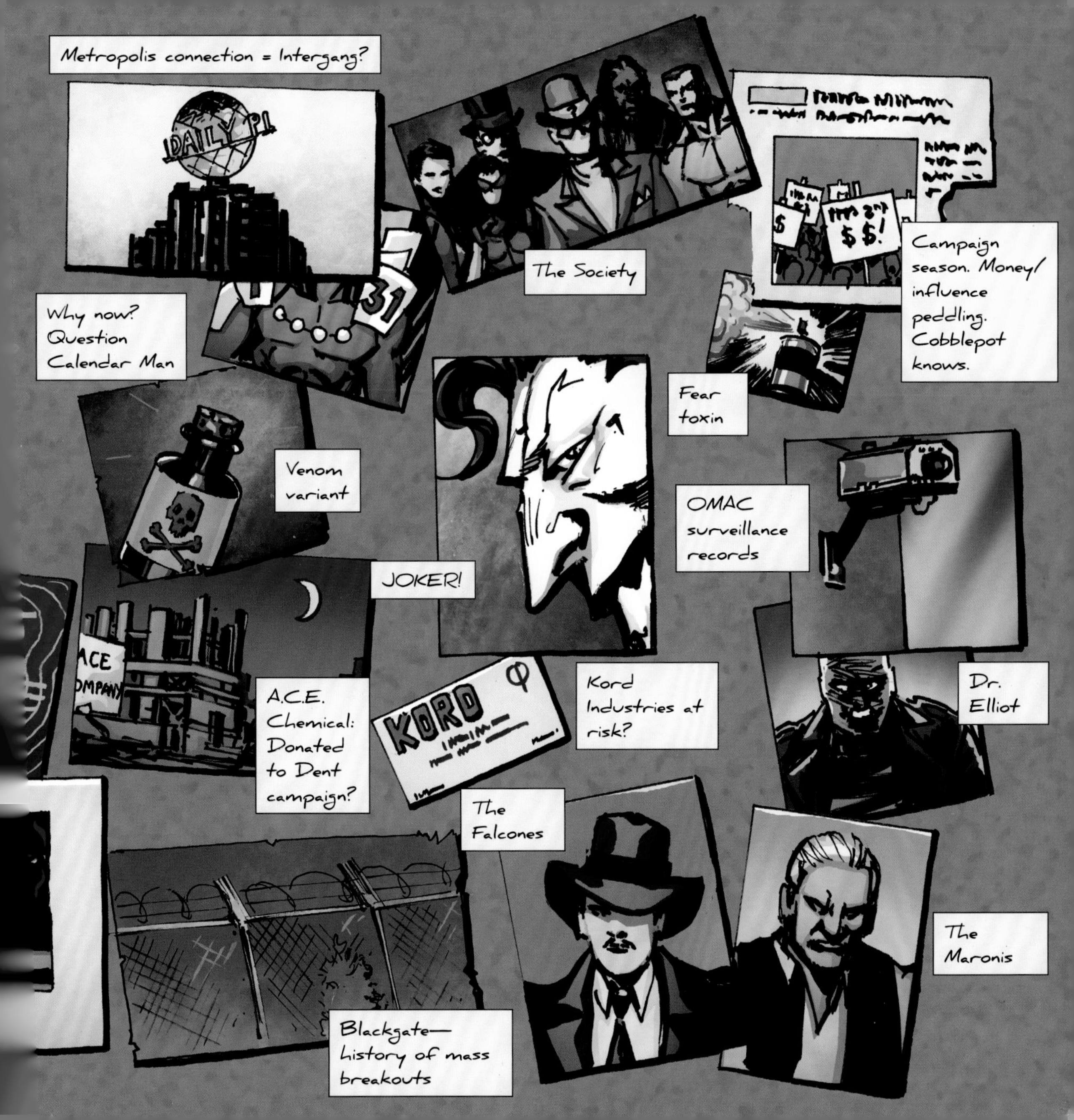
Metropolis connection = Intergang?
The Society
Campaign season. Money/ influence peddling. Cobblepot knows.
Why now? Question Calendar Man
31
$ $!
Fear toxin
Venom variant
OMAC surveillance records
JOKER!
ACE
KORD
A.C.E. Chemical: Donated to Dent campaign?
Kord Industries at risk?
Dr. Elliot
The Falcones
The Maronis
Blackgate—history of mass breakouts

METHODS OF ESCAPE

MASTERING THESE ESSENTIAL TECHNIQUES will ensure you are never kept out of commission for long.

ESCAPING FROM A LOCKED CELL

1. Weaken the wall, not the bars—use acid spray or sonic drill

2. Brace back against solid surface and kick out the base of one bar

3. Use leverage to bend bar and create a sufficient gap

ESCAPING FROM A STRAITJACKET

1. If there is no slack in the straitjacket, dislocate shoulder (Rama Kushna meditative trance achieves this without injury)

2. Pull arm up and over head

3. Unbuckle sleeves with teeth

ESCAPING FROM HANDCUFFS

1. Remove lockpick on Utility Belt or those in either gauntlet

2. Magnetize your glove's fingertips (to prevent dropping the lockpick) and open cuffs

3. Alternative: Weaken hinge of cuffs by scraping on rough surface, apply leverage to pry open

ESCAPING FROM A FLOODING ROOM

1. Rebreather on Utility Belt offers 1+ hour of air; holding your breath should be sufficient for 5+ minutes

2. Look for places where the water is draining; those are weak points

3. Use the weight of the water to your advantage, dislodging stones and creating breaks in the walls or glass; slip through break and follow current to safety

ESCAPING FROM A CRASHING AIRCRAFT

1. Activate your cape's rigidity framework

2. Glide down to rooftop level

3. Aim and fire at rooftop with grapnel gun

4. Retract grapnel and draw yourself to a safe perch

ESCAPING FROM WILD DOGS

1. Disorient the pack—use smoke bomb, flashbang grenade, or hypersonic squealer

2. Target pack leader first—intercept its bite with your forearm gauntlet

3. Roll backward and push your legs into its underbelly, vaulting it into the air

(NOTE: The Joker often employs hyenas and jackals.)

BATMAN'S NETWORK OF ALLIES

I DO NOT place my trust in others blindly. So when I tell you that these individuals are some of your closest confidantes in your war on crime, you know the strength of that bond. Don't shut them out. You need their help, and they need yours.

BATGIRL

No one on Earth is better at navigating computers and data systems than Barbara Gordon. Daughter of Gotham City police commissioner James Gordon, Barbara has recently returned to crime fighting after recovering from a spinal injury inflicted by the Joker. She still possesses the exuberance and overconfidence of youth, but any field inexperience is more than made up for with her electronic expertise. Batgirl possesses an eidetic memory and never forgets any detail she encounters at a crime scene.

BATWOMAN

Kate Kane is ex-military and an asset as a combat strategist. As Batwoman she relies on the Kane family fortune to fund her crusade, much in the same way that Wayne Industries provides Batman's financial backing. Batwoman prefers to work alone, but she will never fail to assist if called upon.

JUSTICE LEAGUE

The Justice League is a Super Hero task force originally formed to thwart an invasion from the extra-dimensional world of Apokolips. Its members are now your teammates. Besides Superman, the following heroes comprise the Justice League's core roster.

WONDER WOMAN
SKILLS: Supernatural strength, speed, and flight
WEAPONS: Lasso of Truth, bullet-deflecting wrist gauntlets, tiara that can be used as a throwing weapon or knife
WEAKNESSES: Magical artifacts, particularly Ancient Greek

GREEN LANTERN
SKILLS: Uses willpower to fly, form protective shields, and generate hard-light constructs
WEAPONS: Power ring
WEAKNESSES: Fear, loss of concentration

CYBORG
SKILLS: Ability to interface with any computer or electronic system
WEAPONS: Can shape metallic parts of body into weapons, including sonic cannon
WEAKNESSES: Signal jamming, software corruption

AQUAMAN
SKILLS: Enhanced strength and toughness; telepathic communication with sea life; can survive underwater indefinitely
WEAPONS: Trident
WEAKNESSES: Extended separation from the ocean's waters limits Aquaman's powers

THE FLASH
SKILLS: Uses the power of the Speed Force to move at incalculable speeds and vibrate through solid objects
WEAPONS: High-tech costume that eliminates friction and generates a protective electrical field
WEAKNESSES: Distraction

NOTE: Superman is the de facto leader of the Justice League, an organization on which you automatically hold a seat.

SUPERMAN
Clark Kent is a close friend and an excellent partner. His Kryptonian heritage gives him the gifts of flight, invulnerability, and long-range heat vision. When combined, those powers make him a powerhouse capable of steamrolling over the opposition. Superman is even more effective, however, when steered by Batman's precision tactics. Because Gotham City and Metropolis are neighbors, you may find yourself collaborating with Superman to track down villains.

THE WAY FORWARD

YOU WOULD NOT be reading these words if I didn't believe you were ready. The world needs a Batman, and that Batman will be you. Fight, but do not become ruthless. Show compassion, but do not grow soft.

It was never my legacy. I did what I did to honor the legacy of my parents. In turn, you will honor me and my parents through your actions as Batman. You have already made me proud. I love you, son.

Now become who you were born to be. Become Batman.

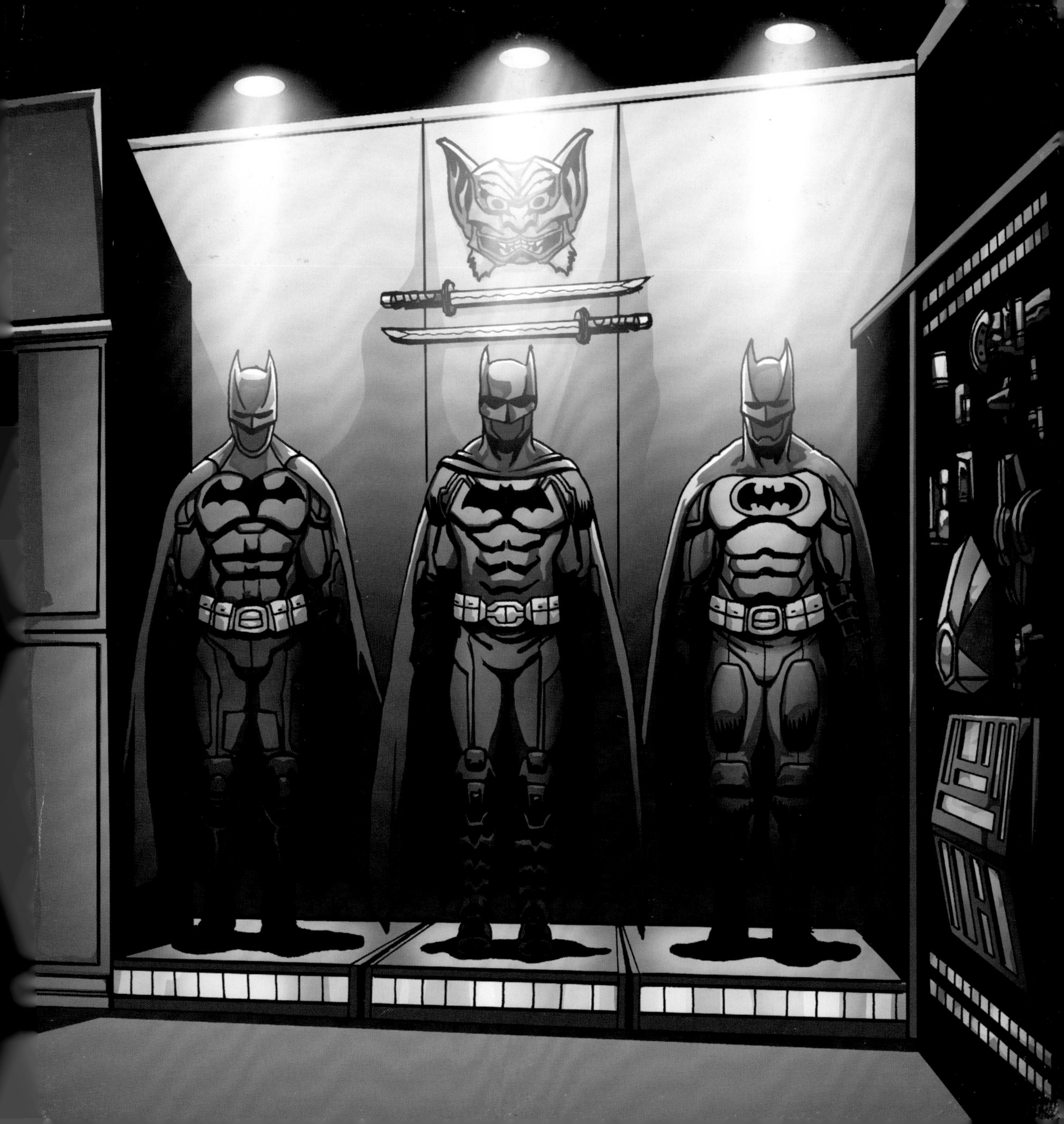

INSIGHT EDITIONS

PO Box 3088
San Rafael, CA 94912
www.insighteditions.com

Find us on Facebook: www.facebook.com/InsightEditions
Follow us on Twitter: @insighteditions

Library of Congress Cataloging-in-Publication Data available.

ISBN: 978-1-60887-418-7

ROOTS of PEACE   REPLANTED PAPER

Insight Editions, in association with Roots of Peace, will plant two trees for each tree used in the manufacturing of this book. Roots of Peace is an internationally renowned humanitarian organization dedicated to eradicating land mines worldwide and converting war-torn lands into productive farms and wildlife habitats. Roots of Peace will plant two million fruit and nut trees in Afghanistan and provide farmers there with the skills and support necessary for sustainable land use.

Manufactured in Hong Kong by Insight Editions

10 9 8 7 6 5 4 3 2 1

ABOUT THE INSIGHT LEGENDS SERIES

Insight Legends is a collectible pop culture library featuring books that take an in-depth look at iconic characters and other elements from the worlds of comics, movies, television, and video games. Packed with special items that give the books an immersive, interactive feel, the series delivers unparalleled insight into the best-loved characters in popular culture and the worlds they inhabit.

PUBLISHER Raoul Goff
ACQUISITIONS MANAGER Robbie Schmidt
EXECUTIVE EDITOR Vanessa Lopez
SENIOR EDITOR Chris Prince
ART DIRECTOR Chrissy Kwasnik
DESIGNER Jenelle Wagner
PRODUCTION MANAGER Anna Wan
PRODUCTION EDITOR Rachel Anderson
EDITORIAL ASSISTANT Elaine Ou

INSIGHT EDITIONS would like to thank Josh Anderson, Elaine Piechowski, Patrick Flaherty, Larry Ganem, and Andrew Marino.

WRITTEN BY Daniel Wallace
ILLUSTRATIONS BY Joel Gomez
ADDITIONAL ART BY Doug Stambaugh: Pages 11, 12, 16, 17, 18, 19, 20, 22, 23, 24, 25, 36, 38, 40, 50, 51, 58, 59, 62, and 63.
COLOR BY Beth Sotelo
COVER ILLUSTRATION AND COLOR BY Freddie E. Williams II